LEVEL
3

D1103116

Coral Reefs

Kristin Baird Rattini

NATIONAL GEOGRAPHIC

Washington, D.C.

Published by Collins
An imprint of HarperCollins*Publishers*
The News Building
1 London Bridge Street
London
SE1 9GF

Browse the complete Collins catalogue at
www.collins.co.uk

In association with National Geographic Partners, LLC

NATIONAL GEOGRAPHIC and the Yellow Border Design are trademarks of the National Geographic Society, used under license.

Second edition 2018
First published 2015

ISBN 978-0-00-831725-6

10 9 8 7 6 5 4 3 2

Printed by GPS, Slovenia

If you would like to comment on any aspect of this book, please contact us at the above address or online.
natgeokidsbooks.co.uk
cseducation@harpercollins.co.uk

Paper from responsible sources

Since 1888, the National Geographic Society has funded more than 12,000 research, exploration, and preservation projects around the world. The Society receives funds from National Geographic Partners, LLC, funded in part by your purchase. A portion of the proceeds from this book supports this vital work. To learn more, visit http://natgeo.com/info.

Table of Contents

City Under the Sea

This shallow sea looks calm. But under the surface, a coral reef is a busy place.

Many thousands of different creatures swim and hide along the reef. There they find food and shelter. They make their home in this "city under the sea".

A coral reef is a very important ecosystem. More sea creatures live around coral reefs than in any other part of the ocean.

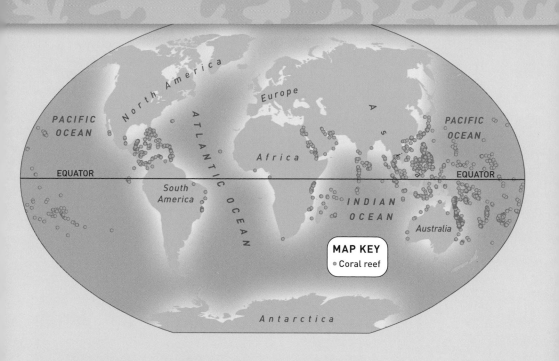

Reefs are found in many spots around the world. Most reefs grow in shallow, clean ocean waters on either side of the Equator. They need sunlight and warm temperatures all year to survive.

Reef Talk

ECOSYSTEM: all the living and non-living things in an area

EQUATOR: the imaginary line around Earth, halfway between the North and South Poles

Reef Builders

a group of
coral polyps

a coral polyp
up close

Coral reefs
look as if they are
made of rocks. But, in fact, they are
groups of animals called corals.
Each coral group is made up of many
separate coral polyps.

In reef ecosystems, there are two kinds of coral: hard and soft. Only hard coral polyps form reefs. Hard coral polyps are named for their hard casings.

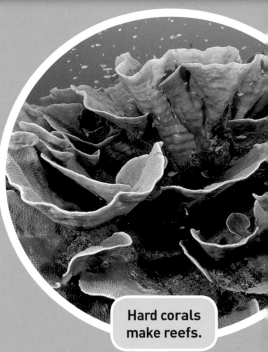

Hard corals make reefs.

Soft corals do not make reefs.

Reef Talk

CORAL POLYP: a small, simple sea animal with a tube-shaped body and a mouth with tentacles at the top

One coral polyp can be as small as the head of a pin. But when many polyps join together, they make a reef that can stretch for many kilometres.

fan coral with open polyps

New polyps build their hard skeletons on top of old ones. Over many years, these layers of skeletons slowly grow into a coral reef.

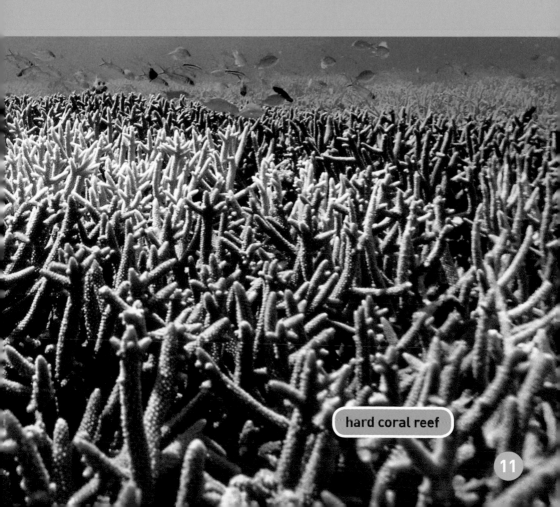

hard coral reef

11

In the Zone

All coral reefs have three zones. The reef flat zone often stretches towards land. The crest zone is the highest part of the reef. The reef slope zone faces the open sea. It's the deepest part of the reef.

reef flat zone

Coral Reef Zones

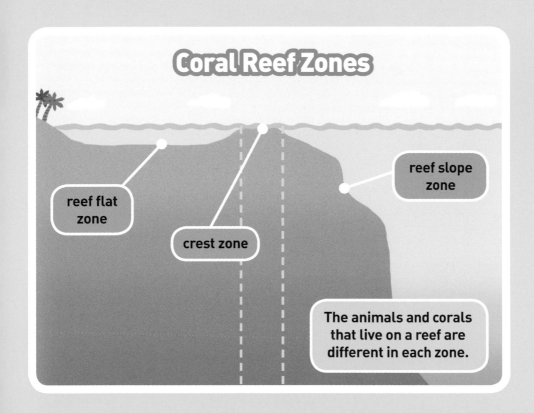

reef slope zone

reef flat zone

crest zone

The animals and corals that live on a reef are different in each zone.

crest zone

reef slope zone

Neighbours on the Reef

Big and small creatures can be found living on coral reefs around the world. Starfish travel slowly along a reef's surface. Giant clams rest there too. Tube sponges stretch up from a reef like small chimneys. Seahorses wrap their tails around pieces of coral. Sea turtles swim around reefs. Eels hide in a reef's cracks.

starfish

tube sponges

seahorse

giant clam

Many animals use camouflage to hide along the reef. Some use it to stay safe from other animals that could eat them. Others use it to hide while they hunt.

Reef Talk

CAMOUFLAGE: an animal's natural colour or shape that helps it hide from other animals

reef stonefish

trumpetfish

cuttlefish

A stonefish's bumpy body blends in with the coral. A trumpetfish dives down and holds still. Its long, thin body stretches up like a tall sponge. A cuttlefish can change its shape and skin colour to match the coral reef.

Reef Plants

The plants that live on coral reefs are very important.

Tiny plants called algae live inside the coral polyps' soft bodies. The algae use sunlight to make food for the coral. This helps the coral to grow.

algae that grow inside coral polyps, as seen through a microscope

Sea grass can grow in the reef flat zone. It helps trap mud from rivers that flow into the ocean. Sea grass also provides food for dugongs and sea turtles.

Reef Talk

ALGAE: simple plants without stems or leaves that grow in or near water

dugong

19

The Reef in Darkness

longspine squirrelfish

As night falls, life along the reef changes. Different animals come out to find food.

octopus

Caribbean reef sharks

cone snail

Squirrelfish use their large eyes to search for shrimp in the darkness. Octopuses stretch their arms over the reef to feel for food. Sharks hunt for fish. Cone snails catch fish and worms.

6 COOL FACTS
About Coral Reefs

1 There are more than 800 different kinds of hard coral in the world's oceans.

2 Brain corals can live for 900 years.

3 The first coral reefs on Earth formed 240 million years ago, before dinosaurs were alive.

Most coral reefs today are between 5,000 and 10,000 years old.

4

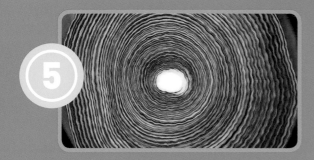

5

Corals have growth rings, just like trees.

The Great Barrier Reef is off Australia's northeast coast. It is the largest coral reef system on Earth. It can be seen from space!

6

People and Reefs

Coral reefs are not only important to animals and plants. They are important to people, too.

Millions of people eat the fish that live around reefs.

Q Which coral is the smartest?

A A brain coral!

Many people earn money from fishing or taking tourists to visit reefs.

Reefs also help to protect people and houses on land. They block big waves from crashing on the shore.

Rescuing Reefs

dead coral

Many reefs are in danger. Scientists are worried about threats to coral reefs.

Ocean waters around the world are getting warmer. Coral polyps die when the water is too warm.

Pollution sometimes spills into the oceans. It can harm reefs.

Large ships and small boats can also damage fragile reefs.

Reef Talk

POLLUTION: harmful things that make water, soil or air dirty

The *Shen Neng 1* struck the Great Barrier Reef in 2010. The ship scraped along the reef for almost two miles, damaging coral and spilling oil into the water.

But there is good news. Many people are working to save reefs.

Volunteers help to clean up pollution on land and at sea. Some countries have special areas where coral reefs are protected.

If you get the chance to visit a coral reef, you can help too! Make sure you look but don't touch.

QUIZ WHIZ

How much do you know about coral reefs? After reading this book, probably a lot! Take this quiz and find out.

Answers are at the bottom of page 31.

1

What are coral reefs made of?

A. hard coral polyps
B. rocks
C. soft coral polyps
D. none of the above

2

Which zone is found on the highest part of the reef?

A. the reef flat zone
B. the crest zone
C. the reef slope zone
D. the end zone

Which of these animals does not live along a coral reef?

A. eel
B. horse
C. starfish
D. giant clam

3

Which of these animals can be found along reefs at night?

A. cone snail
B. octopus
C. shark
D. all of the above

Earth's largest coral reef system is off the coast of which country?

A. Australia
B. Belize
C. Indonesia
D. United States

How old are most coral reefs today?

A. 5,000 to 10,000 years old
B. 50,000 years old
C. 500,000 years old
D. 500 million years old

What can be harmful to coral reefs?

A. ships
B. pollution
C. rising water temperatures
D. all of the above

Glossary

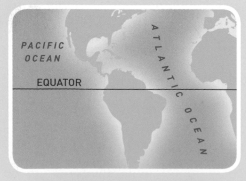

ALGAE: simple plants without stems or leaves that grow in or near water

CAMOUFLAGE: an animal's natural colour or shape that helps it hide from other animals

CORAL POLYP: a small, simple sea animal with a tube-shaped body and a mouth with tentacles at the top

ECOSYSTEM: all the living and non-living things in an area

PACIFIC OCEAN

EQUATOR

ATLANTIC OCEAN

EQUATOR: the imaginary line around Earth, halfway between the North and South Poles

POLLUTION: harmful things that make water, soil or air dirty